The Phoenix of a Mushin Girl

A rebirth story of a teenager

PELUMI WHOLE

WestBow Press books may be ordered through booksellers or by contacting:

WestBow Press
A Division of Thomas Nelson & Zondervan
1663 Liberty Drive
Bloomington, IN 47403
www.westbowpress.com
844-714-3454

ISBN: 978-1-6642-5628-6 (sc)
ISBN: 978-1-6642-5629-3 (e)

Library of Congress Control Number: 2022901852

Print information available on the last page.

WestBow Press rev. date: 02/16/2022

WESTBOW
PRESS®
A DIVISION OF THOMAS NELSON
& ZONDERVAN

Contents

Preface

It is Christmas season of 2021, starting December 20th, I have this overwhelming need to write, I think at first a journal, but no, the urge is stronger than that, maybe a blog, but no the urge is stronger than that too…

Then it hits me, I want to write the book, the one I said I would write is 5-10 years from now when I have a wealth of wisdom to share. This need to write transcends time, it defies the idea I need a wealth of knowledge to share my story, my inner most struggles and journey. I realize also it does not need to be perfect and I can write my book in a week.

So, the journey begins, I write, and this book is the result of that urge to write.

I journey back to my 17-year-old self, it is a tale of self-discovery.

> "Sometimes we need to go back to where it all began and walk forward from there with the knowledge we have now in the present"
>
> ~Pelumi Whole

Prologue

I am in my apartment, but my heart is not in it. My mind keeps wandering back to 2003, I believe that was 2nd level year in Babcock University, Nigeria. I was pursuing my bachelor's in computer science. So, I thought.

Hmm...maybe, I was pursuing something else as well without consciously knowing I was. I was a teenager trying to understand myself. I was a young, open-minded, and curious teenager. It was my second time away from home or should I say away from my Mum. The first time away from home was boarding school at Queen's college where I was for 6 years except holiday breaks.

In my reflective mode, it seemed to me that I was discovering myself in those years. I wanted to discover for myself who I was away from my Mum's definition of me or who she wanted me to be.

In college, I am intrigued by the new experience and exposure. I meet new people and instantly connect with my tribe of introverts and focused nerds (bookworms), library going regular customers. I remember being drawn to a beautiful soul with exceptionally long hair called Arin. We immediately bond as we share a dormitory space. We both were studying computer science. Arin studied a few months at Babcock and soon announced she was going to the United States of America to further her education.

Twenty years after, Arin and I are still good friends as we reconnect again in the US in 2010. Today, we spoke about her visiting me in my apartment. Arin is a doctor now; I am an Agile Coach. An Agile what????.... Let us leave that till my chapter on career.

Dancing

It is another day, and I am still curious about why my heart keeps wondering back to my time in Babcock University. I think it is because today I start dance classes with Alex. I am learning foxtrot, Bachata, Tango and Rumba.

This reminds me of the time I connected with dance in my second year of college at Babcock university. I remember my dance partner, Dapo. I remember rehearsing and dancing Salsa to a group of excited students during a department event. I danced and I remember wearing a pretty dress, I think…my memory might be fuzzy; however, I have pictures of the event tattooed to my mind, propelling me to dance again now.

Dancing now to me is helping me connect back to who I am. I am a creator at heart, I am happy when I dance and I know I will not dance with anyone I perceived as unsafe, because dancing is sacred to me. I also feel alive and my best self when I dance.

> *"There is a bit of insanity in dancing that does everybody a great deal of good"*
>
> ~Edwin Denby

Soul Mate

December 22nd, 2021

I am looking forward to wrapping up work today because I have somewhere to be. Do I really???

Yes, I must be with myself and finish a book called "Triggers" by Marshall Goldsmith. This book talks about how the environment could trigger a particular behavior or response.

As I look back to my years at Babcock college, I see how the environment shaped my naïve and unexposed heart. College was sometimes called a glorified boarding house. We had rules, lights out, expectations on conduct were enforced. I was a rule abider and so I never was really exposed to the real world where people break, bend and exploit rules. This leads to a big heart break in my adult years. I am heart broken and my heart then goes cold.

Yet, one thing keeps that cold heart warm on the inside. It is a memory of meeting my soul mate in college.

What is a soul mate?...

I just learnt this yesterday from a video on Instagram. In the video a young girl asks her Dad what soul mate means, and he tells her with such grace:

"A soulmate is a best friend but more. One person in the world that knows you better than anyone else. Someone who inspires you to be a better person. Soulmate is someone who you carry with you forever. Soulmate is the one person who accepted you and knew you and believed in you before anyone else did. You would always love them no matter what, nothing could ever change that"

I think as God's children, falling in love with him and understanding his plans for us, makes him our soulmate. When I look at my children, I see them as my soul mate because I will love them no matter what.

I guess you're expecting to know more about my college soul mate, so let us get back to that story. It was my second year in college, and I got a pull, let us just say a spiritual pull to want to know God more and deepen my relationship with him. I have always had a thing for having mentors -you know people who have walked the path you want to walk. Mentorship for me is getting another wiser perspective to life.

My college mentor, who helped me grow closer to God and learn to pray more intimately with God, fell in love with me during our prayer sessions. At the time, my relationship with God seemed to be more important so I was focused on that till one day…mentor stepped out in faith and made a bold move of asking me to be his girlfriend. I remember that day at a restaurant and I remember the sparkle in his eyes.

To him, it might have just been a game, hot girl, I get to experiment with, or he felt an emotional pull too, however to me, it was another level of self-discovery, which got interwoven with my search for meaning and connection with God and discovering what love means. It became a very confusing time for me but in the confusion a soulmate was discovered, I did not know at the time until now when I learnt what soul mate means.

I carry that experience in my most intimate memories for almost 20 years. It almost seems like the encounter shaped who I have become. My soulmate may not have connected with me as I did to him however that connection is one that somehow inspired me, and I believe will inspire me for the rest of my life. He saw something in me, I did not see in myself back then. Years after, I am becoming what he saw. His written words still inspire me till date.

For some like myself, your soulmate might never be your spouse, but you carry them in your heart forever. I thought I was weird but, I am not the only one.

Andi, my colleague, and friend says she knows a lot of people who have soulmates they do not talk to but still connect to in a deep way.

The power of the pen

December 22nd, 2021 (nighttime)

It is an interesting evening on December 21st, I am in a coaching session and asked to come up with a topic for discussion. I immediately sense, this is going to be one of those moments when I would put my mind on stage and interrogate my mind.

So, I come up with the topic- "Why do I feel compelled to write a book now?" (This book). A few things become clear to me in the session. Writing is a form of healing for me, so in one sense I write for myself. In another sense, writing is how I connect my thoughts with my environment, reality, and my world. Finally, I would love my great grand kids to find my words, thoughts, and values when I am dead and gone or too old to articulate them well.

My passion for writing started for me when I was about nine years old. Till date, my father reminds me of a moving letter I wrote to him while he was away from home and how he connected so well with my words. FYI…I cannot remember what I wrote but I remember wanting to express my love for him through my words, my pen and the letter. When I was sixteen years old, I also remember I once had a boy friend (My first) who liked to write poems. I remember wanting to keep up, so I wrote poems to him in return. Then later, my writing skills seemed to evolve from love poems to my boyfriend to writing about my experiences and life in a dairy. I ensured I had a dairy every year and I wrote in it. I would say I journaled a lot.

I am 35 years old now and I still journal. I have different journals for different things. I have a thanksgiving journal where I write three things, I am grateful for each day. I have a journal for the terrible experiences I had in a failed marriage, I have a forgiveness journal, I have a journal for the divorce process, I have a journal for my prayers to God over the years.

Now I see the power of the pen for me is HEALING. Writing heals me in a unique way. It refreshes my mind.

"IF YOU WANT TO CHANGE THE WORLD,
PICK UP YOUR PEN AND WRITE"

~ Martin Luther

Being Mum

I am in my apartment at 7am in the morning listening to Alexa sing top Christian music. My spirit is at peace, and I feel this urge to look at myself in the mirror. Impromptu impulses like this are no longer strange to me, it reminds me of who I was as a teenage girl. I was constantly checking myself out. It was like I could not get enough of admiring my beauty both internally and externally.

I am now no more that teenager, I am a Mum to two beautiful, amazing children. Being Mum has been breathe taking, roller coaster, incredible yet stressful, fulfilling and taking the life out of me at the same time. My children are my best gifts from God. He blessed me with such healthy, wise, gifted, confident and inspiring children.

As I look in the mirror this morning in my apartment at 7am, I see my children in me. I see how they transformed me from the selfish teenager to the selfless Mum. The Mum who would move mountains to put a smile on her babies' face. To show how much she loves them. As I proclaim my love for my children, I realize it wasn't that way in the beginning of my first birth.

My first child is a girl who I labored 27 hours to push out into the world. I had nothing to eat but ice cubes all 27 hours. The pain was excruciating, I was tired but when my sweet, beautiful, take-my-time-to-come-into-the-world baby arrived and I heard her first cry for her Mum, something in my world shifted. She was worth every pain, every struggle, every hour of pushing because she was perfect. I cried on first sight of her and fell in love on first sight. My Zion, my Queen.

Then comes my struggle with breastfeeding, my baby girl. I had some form of post pregnancy drama. I wanted my twin towers to be mine only and here is my little one demanding my body part with all entitlement. It took me a while to adjust. This process helped me know and understand the love of a mother is one that keeps giving even at the expense of their own life. It is one of sacrifice and being a servant leader. No wonder by my second birth, I changed careers and became a scrum master also known as servant leader on the scrum team.

My second birth is easier, I am better prepared this time and my son is also very eager to come into the world. He slides out and right past the full grasp of the delivery doctor. It took a wake-up call telling the doctor not to drop the baby. This baby seems really excited to come into the world. My son, my Bobo is great. He is perfect. We bond quickly and he immediately knows ways to push my buttons and get what he needs, my love.

Bobo's birth and life has showed me that one's destiny is not in the hands of another man's thoughts of you or in the labels the world tries to stick or throw at you. One's destiny is in one's own hands. You get to choose who you want to be; you get to know what you want out of life, and you get to choose to live the life you want. I would like my children to live the life they choose, not the life I want for them or choose for them. My prayer is as Mum, I help them to make more good choices than bad and show them the life of love and truth through my own life. The choosing and choices made is fully theirs to make.

Being Mum to Zion and Bobo heals me from my childhood trauma's. It heals me in deep ways. I get to make choices on how I want to raise my children. I get to take the good and bad from my childhood and use that to love and propel my children to understanding themselves, loving self and believing God has great plans for them. My children at this time are 10 and 6 years grown. I find myself learning to listen more as they form their own world views. My role is slowly moving from caregiver to coach and confidant.

"A mother is someone who dreams great dreams for you, but then she lets you chase the dreams you have for yourself and loves you just the same."

~Author Unknown

The Phoenix

I watch the newer version of the Mulan story in 2021 with my children. I remember seeing the phoenix and realizing my life story is like Mulan's. Knowing I am made for more and hiding my true self to earn a seat at the table and then discovering that the phoenix knows my true self and wants to help me earn my seat at the table using my true identity.

I did some research on the phoenix to validate the connection I felt to it. The phoenix is a mythical bird with many tales about it. The one I choose to use is the Chinese west version, where the phoenix is linked to the concept of being reborn and having eternal life. In some ways, in the movie - Mulan, the phoenix is also a guardian, helping Mulan rise to a place of power and overcome the darkness. The phoenix today means one emerging from an old self to a new self.

The teenage Pelumi (Me) who lived in Mushin was embarrassed about it but was bold enough to venture outside her neighborhood to experience life and mingle with people from wealthy homes and understand an unfamiliar perspective. I lived a shielded life; you would think living in a poor neighborhood growing up would expose me to the depts of evil that resides in man. My life was shielded because I always found ways to stay safe, I went to a boarding house for six years, then got into college which was also a boarding house with stricter rules that kept most evil far from me. Everyone I met then acted decent, there were no traumas or drama. Home was where the drama was for me and being in college helped me escape it.

Looking back 20 years from then, my old self did not get the tools it needed or the lessons on life I needed to help me navigate the realities of the real world. The world where there are no rules and if there is a rule, people ignore it or make up their own rules. I was not prepared for an evil world, a world where there are people looking to take advantage of your innocence, steal from you, rob you and disappear. In the last 20years, I have been duped of over $30,000, I have been lied to over one thousand times, I have been deceived by church going pretentious men and women who claim to be Christians.

Recently, I realized I married a man for the potential he presented to me and did not check in with his reality. The shielded- world-is-a-safe-place mentality from my teenage years did not serve me well in my adult years. Once reality caught up with me, I divorced him but then the scars is still there, lessons learnt and two children to fight for.

How does the phoenix fit into this picture?

Remember the phoenix is a representation of a rebirth, a powerful guardian, and an emergence of a new self. Somehow, as I look back over all the incidents and the order they happened, I realize there has always been an element of surprise, divine intervention, and miracles I did not have power over.

I know for certain who my phoenix is. I know because I feel him and in my exceptionally low moments, my heart beats, in my cry, my heart smiles, in my pain, my heart is hopeful.

I feel the phoenix most at church, when I worship, when I pray and when there is an element of surprise in my day. I see the phoenix when I read my bible, I hear the phoenix in worship songs that play on the Alexa app or on you tube.

The phoenix has helped me understand the world from a different lens, hence rebirthing me anew. My phoenix is Jesus Christ.

Mushin

I am in my kitchen reflecting on my life, then it hits me like a block of bricks that my relationship with Mushin has been one of hid and seek.

Part of the early first two decades of my life on earth was about hiding the fact that I grew up in Mushin. Why is this a big deal for me you ask?

Let me walk you down Pelumi's memory lane. I became conscious of where I lived during an event I clearly remember till date. While at Queen's college for my secondary education in Lagos, Nigeria, I meet these set of cool girls called "Bublers". They were smart, classy, rich parents, traveling every summer to America. These girls in my small mind at the time, were living the life I dreamed of. So, I wanted to be part of the group, there was just one slight problem, my parents were not rich, I did not live in a rich neighborhood, and I couldn't afford their lifestyle. I decided to charm my way in by visiting one of the girls in her mansion. My mum happened to be the real-estate agent her family used. I asked Mum if she could drop me over at this girl's house and Mum accepted. I am fourteen at this time and I can take care of myself. I wear my best dress and look sharp to impress this girl so I can be deemed worthy to seat on the table of bublers. We talk for a few minutes; she shows me her room and the rooms in the mansion. Then the landline rings (cell phones was not prominent then), her other "Bubler" friends are coming over to pick her to go to the mall. She looks at me with disappointment and says I must go. I am stunned because my Mum had left and I did not have any way to get home after she left, I was hoping new friend could drop me off at home if I could not go to the mall with her.

She asks I call my Mum to come pick me up, so I do. Mum is busy with work and ask I get a bus ride home to Mushin from Shonibare estate, Ikeja were my Bubler Friends mansion is. I ask host if she can have her driver drop me off, she looks at me and says she cannot drop me off at Mushin and she has never taken a bus ride to the slum before. Then it hits me, where I live is as slum and a place to be ashamed of. My day is made worse, as I step out of the mansion into the rain. As I make my way outside for the gates, I see the girls in a car with a driver, driving to the mall. They do not notice me, but I do because the driver rides past a pothole and dirty water splashes over my beautiful dress.

I transitioned from a girl who was ashamed to a girl who was determined to be rich and prestigious. I also was from then on ashamed of where I lived and did not want to tell anyone to come to my house, not anyone I wanted to impress. Only my most intimate friends knew my home and visited.

As I moved on to Babcock university for more education, I went on dates. You would expect that like in American culture or in the movies, the boy comes to pick girl from her home and parents interrogate boy…that was not my life. No…not this girl.

My dates did not come to my house. I always gave the excuse of my parents not wanting me to bring boys to our home or don't want me dating but the real reason was I was ashamed of where I lived. It gets better when my college soulmate, the one mentioned earlier defies my wall of lies, sees my insecurities, and bravely journeys to Mushin to pick me up for dates and drop me safely back home. He somehow made these rides magical for me and the insecurities I felt seemed to disappear when I was with him.

The fairy tale does come to an end. One day, soulmate cannot drop me off, but his sister and her friend offer to help. That day, I recall seating at the back seat of the car listening to the girls talk about how beneath their class the neighborhood was. They ended up dropping me off in another area close to Mushin and I had to find a bus ride back home. The bus rides are horrible. The bus is cramped with more people than it could take as the drivers are trying to maximize profit. Some people on the bus carry animals like chickens, goats and sometimes smelly fish. The bus ride is noisy and has extremely uncomfortable seats. My insecurities are back. I break up with soulmate and life continues.

Mushin…Mushin…Mushin

Mushin is a congested residential area and does not have the best sanitation, it also has low quality housing. I live in a two bedroom on the second floor of the building.

I finish Babcock University; I travel to the UK for master's degree and then move to the USA in 2010. Now, I get a fresh start I tell myself. I choose better environments to live in. I rent a classy apartment in Manchester while in the UK, when I moved to New Jersey, I also have a classy apartment with better sanitation and great ambience. I am not insecure. I invited people to visit and pick me up for dates.

Then in 2011, my insecurities resurface. I am dating this guy who proposes to me on my 25th birthday and I say yes even though I barely knew him, we dated for barely 6 months in the US. My insecurities showed up again, I assumed the choice was simple, I wanted to be in America than be in Mushin or any where else. The proposal also means at some point, I must take my fiancé to my real home, not my classy apartment but my real home, where I grew up, where my Mum still lives for over 25 years, I must take him to Mushin.

I give myself a pep talk. Something like this, "Oh! I am sure this man is marrying me for my intellect, my wit, he is marrying me for who I really am, not where I live." So, I tell him I live close to Isolo area which is true but not the whole truth. Mushin is close to Isolo, but it is Mushin. Why couldn't I just say I live in Mushin? …. My insecurities show up again.

In October of 2011, Fiancé and I travel to Nigeria for the wedding and the night before the actual traditional wedding, we visit my Mum's apartment in Mushin. I have not been there in two years at that point but still am silently ashamed of where I live, where I must call home.

You might be wondering…what did fiancé think? Well, I did not know until five years into the marriage. We have an intense argument one day and he calls me a Mushin girl; he says in various words you were raised in the slum therefore a worthless slum girl. A whole wave of insecurities rush into my heart. For years, Mushin keeps following me, no matter where I go, even in America, even in my Plano mansion in Texas, I am still called a slum girl.

I went into counselling, and I discovered for myself what love, acceptance, and reconciliation of oneself looks like.

I have concluded, *yes*, I am a girl raised in Mushin, I am proud of who I am, where I lived growing up is part of who I am. I am loved for who I am, I am who I am because Mushin lives on in me. Being a Mushin girl is part of my success story.

"Blessed are they who see beautiful things in humble places where other people see nothing"

~Camille Pissarro

Career and Birth of Growing Mind LLC

December 24th, 2021

Most times when people ask me what I do for a living and I say I am an agile coach, the response I get 90% of the time is "Agile What???". What is Agile?

Agile is a mindset built on quick failure and continuous growth. It builds on transparency, inspection, and adaptation. I am drawn to what I do, I see how this mindset has helped me be a better person not just professionally but personally as well.

When you refuse to NOT have a fixed mindset and you see change as a rebirth, a part of your phoenix experience and your existence, then life is much exciting. I teach and coach people at work to adopt and apply the agile values and principles. I also live by them.

My career has evolved beyond my teenage imagination. Now, I have my own business- Growing mind LLC that helps people visualize and implement career transitions into the agile world. I am passionate about growth. It is a fire that ignited as I nurtured my children's growth and, in some sense, nurtured my growth too.

Life is too short to not grow, to not let go of the past and launch into the unknown. It might be scary at first, uncomfortable but to me it is far worse to die with regrets on "What if" or "what would my life have looked like if I had been…." Be bold and step into the person you know you are or want to be.

Loving myself

It is Christmas, I love this time of the year. After Valentine's Day, this is my next favorite celebration. My daughter's favorite holiday is Christmas.

This Christmas is an emotional one for me because Zion finished writing her first published book – "This is me" over Christmas last year and I think the underlying reason I feel emotional is because this year I do not get to spend Christmas with her and Bobo. It is the first Christmas I missed since they were born. We spent the last 9 Christmas together. These are some consequences of divorce however during this time, another kind of love resurfaces for me. This is one I have not felt so strongly since I was in my teens. Lately, I have found my mind wandering back to what teenagerhood was like for me. It is like a piece of the teenage girl in me, needs to be set free to live fully in the adult I am now.

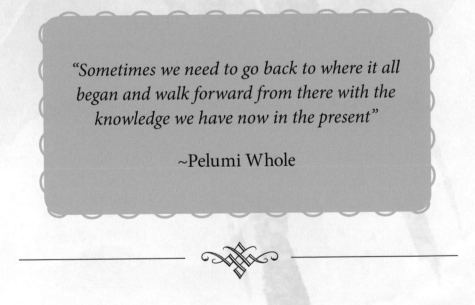

"Sometimes we need to go back to where it all began and walk forward from there with the knowledge we have now in the present"

~Pelumi Whole

My idea of love is convoluted. The concept of love for me, started to form in my teenage years while reading Mills and Boons novels. Mills and Boons were fictional romantic novels I read, and I read a lot of them. They provided me with this picture illusion of love. The fairy tale version, the ever after version where love lasts forever.

Looking back now, I see why I needed romance novels and romantic movies to show me what love was. I did not have good examples of love demonstrated around me while growing up. I had parents who sacrificed for me and ensured myself and my siblings got educated and housed. I am most grateful for this sacrifice but was that love or was it a parental obligation? I had male friends who admired my wit and beauty, was that love or was it attraction and lust? I once married a man who proposed to me, married me, and demanded I be a submissive wife, cultured wife, trophy wife, is that love or is it control?

My quest for love has truly been a convoluted one. This Christmas however that journey comes to its resting place…

Yesterday, I attended Life.Church Christmas Eve Service and the message by Pastor Craig Groeschel is just for me. It starts with Amy Groeschel, Craig's bestfriend and wife praying for the church. Pastor Craig mentioned before he preaches each time, his wife and bestfriend always holds hands with him and prays for him before he gets on stage. In my mind, she is the force behind him, supporting and rooting for him spiritually. Is that love, I wonder?

It gets better, then Pastor Craig preaches on the topic "Does God love me?" and he brings this bear toy he has had since he was a toddler. He mentions how much he loves this bear toy even if the bear is not worth a quarter. He says something profound that strikes me deeply and confirms to me what love is or at least the kind of love I have been searching for my whole life. Pastor Craig says there is a love that loves because the receiver of the love *is valuable* or is worth the love investment.

There is another kind of love that *gives value* to the one it loves or the recipient of the love. Like Pastor Craigs loves his worthless bear because he gives value to it not because the bear is valuable. Love is a choice to give value, respect, service, and honor to someone no matter what.

As I look at my life, I realize I have felt that kind of love only when I am with Jesus. He makes me feel valued. It is his love that has helped me survive the hurt from people who left when they should have stayed, people who cursed when they should have blessed, people who saw no good in a Mushin girl when they should have pulled me closer to discover the rare gem I am.

It is me Jesus loves and loving myself has been possible because I found his love. His love also makes it possible for me to love my children with a love that adds value to the one it loves. Loving myself is a conscious, daily, intentional practice and mindset that allows me to see myself as valued, as one that matters in this world and most importantly as one that is loved by God.

Acknowledgement

Thank you for reading this story.

I acknowledge this is not a typical book, more of a reflective story that I hope inspires you to look at your own story. What happened to you in childhood or teenage years that continually impacts you today?

Travelling back in time and acknowledging the hurt is the door that opens the process for healing. Do not get trapped in the past, use the knowledge you now have to move forward into a new future that opens the door to endless possibilities.

I am grateful for my mentors, women of faith and counselors who provided me with a safe space to explore and interrogate my feelings, thoughts, and actions. I am most grateful to you for sharing life with me.

Finally, my rebirth from the trapped insecure teenage to a Loved Valued Lady would not have occurred if not for the priceless love of my savior, Jesus Christ.

Printed in the United States
by Baker & Taylor Publisher Services